CHINES

Ade

AUTHORED by Nicolas P. Rossenblum
UPDATED AND REVISED by Aaron Suduiko

COVER DESIGN by Table XI Partners LLC
COVER PHOTO by Olivia Verma and © 2005 GradeSaver, LLC

BOOK DESIGN by Table XI Partners LLC

Published by GradeSaver LLC, www.gradesaver.com

First published in the United States of America by GradeSaver LLC. 2015

ISBN 978-1-60259-529-3

Printed in the United States of America

For other products and additional information please visit http://www.gradesaver.com

Table of Contents

Biography of Adeline Yen Mah (1937–)

Adeline Yen Mah was born in Tianjin, China. She lived in Shanghai as a child and from shelter to shelter until settling down in a Hong Kong boarding school at age 11. At age 14, she won an international playwriting competition that convinced her emotionally distant father to allow her to study abroad. Although she had a passion for writing, she attended London Hospital Medical School, graduated as a physician and established a thriving medical practice in California.

After the commercial success of her first novel, *Falling Leaves*, in 1997, Mrs. Yen Mah decided to leave her medical practice to write full time. *Chinese Cinderella* was her second novel, receiving the award from the Children's Literature Council of Southern California in 2000 for Compelling Autobiography and Lamplighter's Award from National Christian School Association in June 2002 for Contribution to Exceptional Children's Literature. She has released two other novels, *Watching the Tree* and *A Thousand Pieces of Gold.*

Adeline is Founder and President of the Falling Leaves Foundation. The mission of her foundation is to promote understanding between East and West and to provide funds for the study of China's history, language and culture. Toward this end, she has started the website to teach Chinese over the internet at no cost to the subscriber.

She is married to Professor Robert A. Mah, with whom she has a daughter; she also has a son from a previous marriage.

Chinese Cinderella Study Guide

Chinese Cinderella is the story of Adeline Yen Mah's youth as the unwanted daughter of a rising businessman in the midst of a great transformation within Chinese society. Adeline's affluent, powerful family considers her bad luck after her mother dies giving birth to her. Life does not get any easier when her father remarries. She and her siblings are subjected to the disdain of her stepmother, while her stepbrother and stepsister are spoiled. Although Adeline wins prizes at school, they are not enough to compensate for what she really yearns for — the love and understanding of her family.

The novel is an abridged version of Mah's first book, *Falling Leaves*, which provides a more detailed look into her years at university in England. Beyond the personal story of Mah's early years, Chinese Cinderella presents a vivid picture of the cultural amalgamation that was early 20th century China thanks to the ramifications of a war-ravaged time. The novel is regarded as an inspiring tale of perseverance and hope, showing the reader the depths of misfortune and the positive opportunities that arise with persistence and work.

Chinese Cinderella Summary

This book is the autobiography of a young Chinese girl, Adeline Yen Mah. Born the fifth child to an affluent Chinese family, her life begins tragically. Adeline's mother died shortly after her birth due to complications bought on by the delivery, marking her as cursed, or 'bad luck', by her siblings. This situation is compounded by her father's new marriage to a young French-Asian woman who has little affection for her husband's five children. Niang proves to be difficult and distant towards all of the children, particularly Adeline, whilst favoring her own younger son and daughter born soon after the marriage. Denied love from her parents, she finds some solace in relationships with her grandfather Ye Ye, and her Aunt Baba, sympathetic-yet-weakened adult figures. Adeline immerses herself in striving for academic achievement in the hope of winning favor from her father, who reacted positively to her medal for academic success.

When the Japanese take over mainland China, her father disappears from their hometown of Tianjin for an extended period of time. Soon after, Niang and her older boy follow. The next couple of months are considered wonderful, since the children are under the care of their grandparents, Nai Nai and Ye Ye. However, Nai Nai's death leads to the return of her father and their move from Tianjin to Shanghai. There, her father has bought a large mansion where the entire family is supposed to live.

After standing up to Niang's ill treatment of Youngest Sister, Adeline suffers the worst at the hands of her stepmother. She is denied carfare, frequently forgotten at school at the end of the day, and whipped for daring to attend a classmate's birthday party against Niang's wishes. Adeline records her entire childhood, through several schools and houses, through the people she meets and one very special duckling pet – Precious Little Treasure (or PLT for short) that she cares for. She records her sister's wedding, her school friends, and her on-going quest for knowledge.

Adeline finds great success at school and gets elected as class president, a time of momentous joy for her and her classmates. However, when her classmates choose to bring the celebration to her house, her parents lash out and threaten to move her to a far away school. Niang's brusque nature and her father's ambivalence shock Adeline's school friends, who rally about her on the next day of school. However, when she gets home, she is shocked to find out that she is being sent to a boarding school in Tianjin immediately. Her ensuing goodbyes with Aunt Baba and Ye Ye are sorrowful, but filled with uplifting words. On the flight over, when filling out her new school enrollment record, her father forgets the spelling of Adeline's Chinese name, adding insult to injury.

Incredibly, her time at her new school (a convent in Tianjin) is capped by its desertion with the inevitable march of the People's Liberation Party. After being inadvertently saved by her lovely aunt from Niang's side of the family, Adeline returns to live with her family, now in Hong Kong. She is quickly sent to another boarding school, Sacred Heart. Even though Adeline is repeatedly moved up to grades above those of her peers, it is only when she wins an international play-writing contest in high school that her father finally takes notice and grants her wish to attend college in England. Despite her parent's heartbreaking neglect, she eventually becomes a doctor and realizes her dream of being a writer.

Chinese Cinderella Characters

Adeline (Jun-Ling/Wu Mei)

Adeline is the fifth youngest of the Yen family and the protagonist of the novel. The book follows her childhood from the age of four to her departure to England in her early teens. Adeline is an outcast in the eyes of much of her own family, since her birth brought upon the death of her mother. Her inadvertent role in her mother's passing causes animosity between her and her older siblings and contributes to her father's apathy towards her.

Adeline maintains a very close relationship with her Aunt Baba and both her grandparents, turning to them for reason and comfort throughout her early years. Her Aunt's support combined with her father's brief flashes of approval lead Adeline to pursue academic excellence, leading to her outstanding performance in school and indomitable drive. Although her siblings and stepmother Niang often abuse her, Adeline attempts to overcome her problematic home life with her performance and community outside it.

Niang (Jeanne Virginie Prosperi)

Niang is the stepmother to Adeline and her four older siblings and the natural mother to 4th Younger Brother (Franklin) and Little Sister (Susan). Niang is married to Adeline's father one year after the death of Adeline's mother, at the age of 17. Father is very proud of his "French" wife, showing her off to friends and treating her to her every whim.

Niang establishes her as the de facto head of the household by the time the family moves to Beijing, setting a clear separation between her natural born children and her adopted ones. This leads to conflict with Father's first four children, with power imbalance and manipulation rendering the conflict toothless. The main dissenter to Niang's power is Adeline, who stands up against the injustices she perceives, unlike her other siblings. However, Adeline is still very much conscious of the power Niang holds over her Father.

While she outwardly expresses respect and deference to the natural head of the household, Ye Ye, for the sake of Father's feelings, their relationship is a frigid one. Likewise, she sees Aunt Baba as a threat, after an incident with Little Sister on the first night in Beijing, and does her best to remove her influence from the household. Niang's personality is fairly static throughout the novel, permanently the antagonist to Adeline's story.

Father (Joseph Yen)

Joseph is the father of Adeline and all of her siblings, referred to as "Father" throughout the novel. Affluent, intelligent, business savvy and ambitious, Father is seemingly ignorant of the feelings of others, particularly his children. Continually abandoning Adeline, ignoring the wishes of his own father, he appears to value only the opinion of his new wife Niang and an overwhelming drive to be materially successful.

However, his distinct aloofness can perhaps be traced back to the death of his mother, Nai Nai. After being away in Shanghai to establish a stable job, his first appearance after returning to Tianjing is distinct for his only outward display of emotion: Adeline notices his reddened eyes from mourning Nai Nai. This is not replicated again, not even at Ye Ye's funeral. Indeed, the aftermath of Nai Nai's death leads to a permanent severance with his Tianjing life, demanding that Aunt Baba burns all pictures of his first wife.

Adeline's relationship with her father stems from a desire for approval, based on his happiness when she earns distinction in her classes. Father's pride makes her feel like a member of the family, pushing her to succeed at academics. Although she notices his apathy towards her on occasion, Adeline's desire to please Father is very prominent in the novel.

Ye Ye

Ye Ye is Adeline's grandfather on her father's side and the head of the household at the beginning of the novel. A devout Buddhist, Ye Ye maintains a moral compass unseen in the rest of the family. Working at the same company as his son, Ye Ye has a tight bond with him. Ye Ye is traditionally seen as the patriarch of the family, but his role is undermined by Niang's introduction to the family. While Ye Ye remains an influence within the household, it's primarily ceremonial, if that.

Ye Ye's relationship with his grandchildren is slight, except in the case of Adeline whom he views as "different." He supports her as best he can, telling Adeline that she has the talent to break out of her unfortunate cycle. In his later years, Ye Ye is visibly saddened by the state of his family and the behavior of his son.

Aunt Baba

The eldest daughter of Ye Ye and Nai Nai, Aunt Baba is described as "meek, shy and unmarried," wholly dependent on her younger brother--Adeline's father--financially. Tasked with taking care of Adeline, the two develop a close bond due to their position as the unwanted and powerless members of the family. Aunt Baba provides encouragement for Adeline to pursue her dreams, a decision that causes her to lose favor in the eyes of Niang.

A constant source of patience and rationality in the tumultuous world of this novel, her separation from Adeline furthers the latter's loneliness and forces her to become more self-reliant. Indeed, the dynamics between Aunt Baba and Adeline and Aunt Baba and Niang serve as the driving factors of the story.

Big Sister (Lydia)

The eldest of Father's original children, Big Sister is vicious, jealous, and spiteful. Born with a lame arm, she uses her handicap to her advantage, by forcing her siblings to carry out her chores. This is just one of the ways she manipulates those around her. Big Sister constantly attempts to curry favor with Niang and Father to advance her own situation. By ratting out her younger siblings, she is invited to join the "superior" children on the second floor, and becomes one of Niang's spies. Though she is one of the cruelest to Adeline, Big Sister is just a lonely girl looking for love and attention.

While on a visit with Father and Niang to Tiajin, Niang arranges Big Sister's marriage to Samuel, a thirty-one year old stranger. Big Sister is thrilled with the idea of marriage, but Adeline is horrified. She cannot imagine being taken out of school at seventeen and "thrust into the arms of a stranger," though Big Sister is overjoyed to have all eyes on her. This is the last we see of Big Sister, as she joyfully leaves for her honeymoon.

Nai Nai

Nai Nai is Adeline's paternal grandmother, the wife of Ye Ye. Born under a different dynasty, her feet were broken and bound as a child. This causes her constant pain and she "hobbles" instead of walking tall. In the few chapters where she's present, Nai Nai is portrayed as a sensible and strong woman, capable even with the handicap imposed on her. The traditional matriarch of the Yen family, the family structure falls apart with her death. Without her support, Ye Ye is no longer able to hold his position at the top of the chain, and Niang takes over the household. Nai Nai's death is a turning point in the novel, from a time of tranquil freedom to an oppressive atmosphere and a segregated home.

Big Brother (Gregory)

Adeline's eldest brother is distinct from the other three in that he often shows a maturity corresponding to his position, albeit interposed with flashes of malice that corrode any of Adeline's built-up good will. Big Brother, along with his other two natural brothers, is forced to have an outdated hairstyle and wear antiquated clothes, leading to much ridicule from their classmates. Although he takes up the banner of rebellion against Niang, his resolve is extinguished by his stepmother's all-encompassing influence.

Big Brother shows flashes of compassion towards his younger siblings and has a bond with his fellow brothers. However, he instigates many of Adeline's misfortunes, as seen in the case of the urine orange juice and the death of PLT. At the end of the day, Big Brother's character is left unsatisfactorily underdeveloped, considering the difficult balance that is expected of him, a leader among his siblings but a subordinate towards an unjust mother.

Second Brother (Edgar)

The cruelest of all Adeline's brothers, Second Brother often goes out of his way to make life miserable for Adeline. He hates when she is praised and always doles out some punishment each time she has some positive attention. Second Brother comes up with many of the tricks they play on Adeline. Our protagonist is always on edge when near him and can find no real reason for his supreme hatred for her; she only knows that her existence is reason enough for the family to hate her.

Third Brother (James)

Third Brother is the youngest of the three brothers born out of Father's first marriage. While he is very close to his two older brothers and is involved in their hijinks, he is portrayed as exceptionally compassionate towards Adeline. Adeline loves her brother for this and often sees him as the most reliable of the bunch. However, she feels betrayed by his conspiracy in the urine-orange juice prank on the day Adeline won a major academic award. Although Third Brother is the closest to Adeline, their relationship is not exceptionally intimate.

Fourth Brother (Franklin)

The oldest child in the Niang/Joseph Yen marriage, Franklin is raised in a different world than his stepsiblings even though they occupy the same house. Always having the most stylish haircuts and modern clothing, Franklin is afforded every amenity that is kept from the others. Franklin's character is not developed beyond his favored status, at least not until the malicious prank he attempts to pull on Ye Ye near the end of the latter's life. Although it is implied that he is spoiled, his cruelness only materializes through this event.

Little Sister (Susan)

The youngest of all the children, she is pampered and well looked after. Niang treats her like an angel and showers gifts on her constantly, making the others jealous. Initially, Little Sister's relationship with Niang was tumultuous, as they were separated for a year and a half. Upon her homecoming, Little Sister didn't recognize her own mother and Niang beat her for her disobedience. After this rocky reunion, Little Sister settled into her role as favorite child. Though she is one of the children given special treatment, Little Sister appears to have more empathy than Fourth Brother, calling him out for his misbehavior when he attempts to hurt Ye Ye.

Schilling Family

A beacon of kindness in an unkind landscape, the Schillings (Aunt Reane, Victor, and Claudine) serve to act as a foil to the harshness of the Yen household. Adeline lauds the ideal brother-sister relationship exhibited by the Schilling children; she wishes very deeply to become part of their family. The Schillings treat Adeline as an equal instead of an outcast, drawing lots to see who sleeps on the ground when Adeline assumed that the unfortunate lot would naturally fall to her. Victor also loudly stands up to Niang's treatment of Adeline, a unique scene of warmth and action within the novel.

Chinese Cinderella Glossary

akimbo

Position in which hands are on hips and elbows are bowed outward.

austerity

Life under difficult economic conditions, poorness.

Buildings on the Bund

The waterfront buildings of Central Shanghai, usually referring to the buildings and wharves along the Zhongshan Road.

C rations

Canned, pre-cooked wet rations issued to the US Marines and passed on to the Chinese after the end of World War II.

Clark Gable, Vivien Leigh, Lana Turner and Errol Flynn

Famous film stars of the 1940's and 50's. Their popularity soared in China with the end of World War II.

Frances Eliza Hodgson Burnett

English playwright and author, best known for *The Secret Garden*, *Little Lord Fauntleroy*, and *The Little Princess* (Adeline's favorite book).

Fuyu persimmons

Squat, non-astringent persimmons that can usually be eaten before ripening, or when they are still firm. Though the persimmons Wu Chun-mei offers the girls are not actually Fuyu persimmons; if they had been, the persimmons would actually have been edible.

General Zhang Fei 張飛

A military general who served under Liu Bei in the late Eastern Han Dynasty. He aggressively fought for Liu Bei in many different campaigns, but was eventually assassinated by his subordinates.

Huangpu River

River flowing through the middle of Shanghai, also the largest river of Shanghai. It was man made during the Warring States Period.

King Lear

Shakespearean tragedy following the title character's descent into madness after he divides up his estate between his daughters. Left with nothing in the end, his plight reminds Adeline of the misfortunes of Ye Ye.

Let it be (Suan Le, 算了)

An expression meaning let it be, let it pass, forget about it. One of Third Brother's favorite expressions and an expression Adeline must learn to live by.

Mandarin Dialect

This is the group of dialects spoken in northern and southwestern China and makes up the largest spoken language in China. Standard Chinese, called "Putonghua" or "Guoyu" in Chinese, which is often also translated as "Mandarin" or simply "Chinese", belongs to this group. It is the official spoken language of the People's Republic of China and one of the official languages of Singapore, but not Taiwan.

Mercurochrome

A topical anesthetic used for cuts and scrapes.

obsequious

Used to describe Miss Chien, the younger children's tutor, this means obedient or attentive to an excessive degree.

Opium War

From 1856-1860, foreign powers (United Kingdom, France, and the United States) fought against the Qing dynasty due to issues of trade. Trade was fairly one-sided and benefited the foreign nations, an imbalance that Chinese citizens wanted to change. The War was won by the foreign invaders, effectively dividing up China among themselves.

People's Liberation Army

The Communist Army, led by Mao Zedong, was the force that took over China from the Nationalist Party during the Chinese Civil War that ended in 1950. The war was a back and forth affair that culminated in the expulsion of the Nationalist to Taiwan. They maintain power to the day.

qipao

Also known as the cheongsam (旗袍), the qipao is a one-piece, traditional Chinese dress that has been popular since the 17th century.

rickshaw

This method of transportation consists of a wheeled cart pulled by one person. The Yen's have a rickshaw in Tianjin, but primarily use a car in Shanghai and Hong Kong.

Shanghai dialect

Also known as the Hu dialect, the Shanghai dialect, or Shanghainese, is derived from the Wu dialect. Shanghainese only has two tones, whereas Mandarin is a contour tonal language.

Three Kingdom's War

Following the fall of the Eastern Han Dynasty, this was a war between three states that claimed succession to the throne; Wei (魏), Shu (蜀), and Wu (吳).

Chinese Cinderella Themes

Acceptance

Adeline's story is that of an unwanted daughter, seeking acceptance within her own family. Although the reader can clearly see the actions of the Yen family as twisted and wrong, it is evident that young Adeline's happiness stems exclusively from the approval of these deeply flawed people. Indeed, Chinese Cinderella shows us that the drive for acceptance does not depend on the quality of the group we seek to belong to; rather, it is innate and entirely encompassing. As the author herself states, "Although this story was written when I was in my late fifties, inside I am still the same little five-year-old yearning for the love of my parents."

Perseverance

Chinese Cinderella is a story of perseverance, of the idea that a "single positive dream is more important than a thousand negative realities." Adeline Yen shows an unnatural resilience throughout her story, a level of composure unbelievable for a child her age. The treatment faced by young Adeline via her family is so jarring that the reader's mind instinctively classifies them as fictional. However, Adeline keeps trudging on past the point where most people would break, insistent on the belief that something good will come from her effort. Perseverance only truly counts when life is at its bleakest, a journey that Adeline undoubtedly undertook.

Self-Worth

Ye Ye best expresses the importance of self-worth in one of his last messages to Adeline, telling her that she can "vanquish the demons only when you yourself are convinced of your own worth." A large part of Adeline's insecurity stems from her belief that the only road towards belonging is the approval of her father and mother. The novel presents her growth as a person as a concurrent development towards self-reliance, ending with Adeline gaining a measure of self-worth. At the end of the day, the opinion of her insensitive father is not what sparks her glee; it is the bright future that she can now create.

Isolation

One of the most powerful scenes in Chinese Cinderella is only partly satisfied through Adeline's point of view. When Adeline is spending Christmas dinner all by herself in the large mess hall at St. Joseph's, it only natural for the reader to picture the ostentatious family dinner that the Yen family must be having in Shanghai. The two images juxtaposed show the utter isolation that was imposed on Adeline, placed in a world where no one truly cares if she lives or she dies. Isolation, be it physical (like Adeline's banishment to Tianjin and the Holy of Holies) or mental (as seen with Adeline's refusal to share her status with Wu Chun-Mei), plays an important role in the development of our characters. Adeline, however, seems to draw strength from these extended periods of isolation. Yen Mah's characters show us how isolation can be overcome if seen as a temporary state, a difficult proposition for those in the midst of it.

Pride

Father's main goal in life is to be admired by his peers for his material wealth and his business accomplishments, often leading to the neglect of his family. While the reader may initially attribute egoism exclusively to the antagonists of Chinese Cinderella, it is important to note that Yen Mah makes a point of showing us the harmful ego within herself. Adeline refuses to ask for rides from her more affluent friends and makes excuses for the state of her clothes because she is too proud to admit that her home life is anything less than perfect. Although our instinct is to tie this in with positive qualities like strength and loyalty, it is the same problem as that which her dad exhibits. The overwhelming desire to be respected by your peers can lead to lies and deceits that paint a picture far different from reality, creating a prideful facade that is privy to collapse.

Loss of Innocence

The growth of Adeline as a character comes with the harsh realization that those who she held up as worthy of praise and adoration did not deserve quite so much of either. Her father's pride is the source of her happiness at the beginning of the novel, but he proves to care so little about his youngest daughter that he does not even know her birth name. Ye Ye--the patriarch of the family--seems untouchable during the time in Tianjin, but cannot stand up to Niang when the family moves. Likewise, Aunt Baba is seen as the protector for a mistreated Adeline yet she does not do anything to prevent her expulsion from the household. While both Ye Ye and Aunt Baba want what is best for Adeline, they do not go out of their way to improve her situation, wary of risking their own comfort. Yen Mah teaches the reader that our heroes are merely people, perhaps not as heroic as we would wish them to be. Adeline eventually learns this and succeeds through her own efforts, not relying on will of others.

Education and Individuality

The importance of education and the character development, independent of the expectations of others, is evident throughout Chinese Cinderella. Adeline manages to work her way out of her dire beginnings through her academic performance and the personality that develops from those endeavors, growing into an outstanding writer thanks to her love of Shakespeare and her passion for storytelling. Her freedom via England came through this talent and her victory in an international playwriting competition. Indeed, a recurring theme in the novel is Adeline's adamant belief that she does not want to end up like her sister, in an arranged marriage with a man twice her age. Adeline's drive to be her own person is crucial to her ultimate success, supplemented by an unquenchable thirst for knowledge.

Chinese Cinderella Quotes and Analysis

"'But then Mama died giving birth to you. If you had not been born, Mama would still be alive. She died because of you. You are bad luck.'"

Chinese Cinderella, p.3

The first lines we hear from Big Sister set the tone of both the novel and the character. The blame that rests on Adeline from her birth prohibits any hope of an easy childhood; with her siblings believing that she brought about the end to their idyllic lives, she is in no position to convince them otherwise. The endless cycle of hate and bias has already begun, fed by any negative turns or disappointing results. Although this is brutally unfair, it--like being a daughter and being Chinese—is a part of realities that Adeline has no choice but to overcome.

"It hurt so badly I couldn't sleep. I screamed in pain and begged my mother to free my feet, but she wouldn't. In fact, the pain has never gone away. My feet have hurt every day since they were bound and continue to hurt today. I had a pair of perfectly normal feet when I was born, but they maimed me on purpose and gave me lifelong arthritis so I would be attractive."

Chinese Cinderella, p.8

The practice of footbinding in Chinese culture was a cruel one that persisted for many centuries and only ceased in the early days of the 20th century. This form of subjugation for Chinese women was on of many ways that a pervasive anti-female culture was ingrained in the Chinese psyche. The belief that women were vastly inferior to males allowed for the ill treatment of daughters and the propagation of arranged marriages, creating an imbalance that would make it difficult for young girls like Adeline to succeed. The history of footbinding through the eyes of Nai Nai and what that meant for women of the day was another disadvantage that Adeline had to overcome while growing up.

"I was winning the medal every week and wearing it constantly. I knew this displeased by siblings, especially Big Sister and Second Brother, but it was the only way to make Father take notice and be proud of me."

Chinese Cinderella, p.15

Adeline's flaunting of the medal can be seen as another show of excessive pride within the novel but it is instead the means through which a young girl looks to gain acceptance within an uncaring family. The pride over that measly medal shows the sadness that is Adeline's day to day, with her siblings hating her achievement and her dad only caring when she receives it. Adeline only truly matures when she realizes that her achievement should only matter if it makes her happy, not her dad. As long as she is stuck in this dependent cycle, Adeline will never be content and independent.

> *"The room was completely still. The only sound I heard was that of Ye Ye chomping on his apple. Surely he was going to say something to put Niang in her place!"*
>
> *Chinese Cinderella, p.39*

The balance of power within the Yen household has shifted dramatically by this point of the novel. What was originally a house run by Father under the supervision of Nai Nai and Ye Ye has become the empire of Niang, with Ye Ye only preserved as a mouthpiece. The importance of this scene is that the shift of power strongly hampers the future of Adeline within the household, especially after the fiasco with Little Sister and Aunt Baba. Without Ye Ye's protective and sympathetic presence holding any sway, Adeline's life is surely going to go from bad to worse.

> *Everyone laughed, including Mother Marie. "And if you could have one wish granted, what would it be?"*
>
> *"To receive a letter addressed to me. Just one letter. From anyone."*
>
> *Chinese Cinderella, p.131*

Adeline's loneliness is exemplified in this quote from her time at St. Joseph's in Tianjin, far away from any family or friends. There is nothing like isolation, especially in cases this extreme. With no one looking for her and no one writing her letter, not even her Aunt Baba, Adeline feels as alone in the world as one can be. The will to keep going even after that shows the perseverance that this book promotes.

> *"My heart gave a giant lurch as her words sank in. For a dazzling moment, I knew with every fiber of my being that somehow, against all odds, Aunt Baba had come to my rescue! The whole of me was vibrating with joy, and I ran as fast as I could towards the visitors' lounge, followed by Mother Marie."*
>
> *Chinese Cinderella, p.136*

The joy exhibited by Adeline when she is given reason to believe that her savior has come at last is heart wrenching. After all the misfortune that has befallen this young girl in her eleven years of life would lead one to believe that something had to break right. In a strange way, something finally did. Even though Aunt Baba, who the reader views as the primary positive adult figure in Adeline's life, had still not taken an active role in helping her situation, the Schillings turned out to be an unexpected blessing. The quote shows the utter joy that our otherwise steadfast protagonist lets break through, a revealing relief after putting on a brave face. As much as Adeline is working hard to not let the unfortunate turns get to her, the outpouring of emotion shows how much she actually needed something to go her way.

> *"You may be right in believing that if you study hard, one day you might become fluent in English. But you will still look Chinese, and when people meet you, they'll see a Chinese girl no matter how well you speak English. You'll always be expected to know Chinese, and if you don't, I'm afraid they will not respect you as much."*
>
> *Chinese Cinderella, p.151*

Ye Ye expresses a level of insight that has been apparent within him for the entirety of the novel but never outwardly expressed until this instance. The quote expresses finality: regardless of all the effort or sweat that Adeline pours onto her goals, there are some inescapable truths that come with her birth. Perseverance is an admirable trait that Adeline exhibits throughout the novel, leading the reader to believe that anything can be overcome with faith and hard work. Ye Ye shows us that diligence doesn't destroy all barriers but rather that some must be first accepted to be overcome.

> *"Above all, there is the wisdom and magic of our language itself. When you read a Chinese book, try to look at the characters and think about them. I have met many who appear to know a good many Chinese words but never actually grasp the true meaning of any of them."*
>
> *Chinese Cinderella, p.151*

This quote by Ye Ye reflects a core principle of Yen Mah's novels, the beauty of the Chinese language. This is followed by a monologue on how the pictographic aspect of Chinese characters can help tell a story in ways that the Western alphabet cannot, reflecting the message of the author's foundation which aims to teach youth of Chinese heritage their language. This also reinforces the theme that people should be seen as much more than what society views them as, a message that is clearly lost on the rest of Adeline's family. Her father understands the importance of appearances and the value of daughters in society, but does not truly grasp the potential that his daughter exhibits until it is shoved in his face, well after all the damage is done.

> *"He climbed out to stand by my side. Together, we watched the car drive off. I was overwhelmed by his chivalry but could find no words sufficient to express my gratitude. After a painful pause, I ran upstairs, dug out my book Paper Magic, gave it to him and said, "This is for you.""*
>
> *Chinese Cinderella, p.156*

Victor is the only person to see the injustices heaped on Adeline for what they are and then take an active role in protesting them. By refusing to get in the car with Niang and the others, Victor vocalized his opposition, something that Ye Ye and Aunt Baba never did. The gift offered by young Adeline can be seen as a means to highlight this distinction; while Aunt Baba and Ye Ye earned a level of loyalty, Victor deserved a higher distinction. The book was the only possession of any value that Adeline had, yet she understood the actions of Victor to be worthy of such high praise. In this exchange, Yen Mah relays the message that, while empathy is valuable, embodying the change is deserving of greater praise.

> *"Contrary to all logic, I had the uncanny sensation that Shakespeare had actually had my Ye Ye in mind when he wrote his immortal play four hundred years earlier."*
>
> *Chinese Cinderella, p.168*

King Lear is a powerful symbol of the tragic relationship that has befallen Ye Ye and his son, a story of a wise old king driven to ruin by the destruction of his family. Although the wedge driven between Father and Ye Ye is not at the center of our novel, it's impact reverberates throughout. While the love between the father and son continues to be strong, the connection is rendered hollow thanks to the sway that Niang has over the direction of the family. The loss of influence that Ye Ye suffers is indicative of the breakdown of what was once an strong family, getting to the point where Adeline is treated like she is. The loss of perspective and the tragedy of Ye Ye's disempowerment are representative of the larger workings of the novel.

Chinese Cinderella Chapter 1-3 Summary and Analysis

Summary

Adeline returns home after the first week of kindergarten glowing with happiness; she has been chosen to lead the class and has received a medal for her work. Aunt Baba is full of pride and files the certificate of achievement accompanying the medal in her safe deposit box as if it was "some precious jewel impossible to replace" (2). While rummaging through the box, Adeline finds a photograph of her grandparents' wedding then asks to see a photo of her deceased mother. Aunt Baba nervously changes the subject.

Mah recounts the history of her family and the background of her home in Tianjin. A year after her mother's death, her father remarried a "seventeen year old Eurasian beauty fourteen years his junior" (4) of French and Chinese ancestry. Soon after, they had two children, resulting in a family of twelve at the Tianjin mansion. Their stepmother, Niang, cares nothing for her stepchildren. That, coupled with the fact that Adeline's siblings "blamed [her] for causing Mama's death and never forgave [her]," (4) makes it difficult for Adeline to advance her place within the family.

The difficulties that Adeline faced in the other aspects of her life show how easy it was for her to latch on and form a deep bond with Aunt Baba: Aunt Baba was tasked with taking care of Adeline, given that role due to her financial dependence upon her brother. The city they reside in, Tianjin, was one of China's costal cities occupied by foreign troops after the Opium War and was heavily influenced by the French concession, "a little piece of Paris transported into the center of a big Chinese city" (5). Even after the bombing of Pearl Harbor and the Japanese occupation of Tianjin, the French Concession was still governed by French officials.

The third chapter provides a snapshot of a normal family dinner in the Yen household. Dinner immediately follows the events in chapter one, so Adeline is proudly wearing her medal as she goes down to the table. Adeline and Aunty Baba are the first to arrive, joined shortly after by Ye Ye and Nai Nai. While Adeline helps Nai Nai to her seat, Adeline curiously asks about Nai Nai's diminutive bound feet. Soon after, the brothers file in, with Second and Third Brother taking their seats on either side of Adeline.

Adeline recollects a story of Big Brother's mischief until Third Brother congratulates her for the medal. Prompted by the praise, Second Brother punishes Adeline, the "ugly little squirt" (9), for her excellence. Soon after, Father, Niang and Big Sister arrive, forcing Second Brother to stop punishing Adeline. The meal commences and family as a whole ignores Adeline, when Father surprised everyone by commenting on her medal. This was "the first time anyone could remember Father… saying anything to [Adeline]"(11). After the meal in their jealousy, the siblings steal Adeline's dessert.

Analysis

This first chapter sets the stage for Adeline's story. Mah uses plain language and simple sentences to invoke the feeling of childhood nostalgia, giving the story a candid air. Mah characterizes her younger self as an innocent and curious girl, eager to please and learn. Aunt Baba's pride and patience with Adeline creates the illusion that they come from a loving house.

The way that Aunt Baba treats Adeline's certificate like "some precious jewel" (4) shows how Aunt Baba vies Adeline as a treasure "impossible to replace" (4). In the final paragraph of Chapter 1, this illusion is shattered. Big Sister's treatment of Adeline is representative of the rest of the family's opinion; Adeline is the sole cause of her mother's death and is "bad luck." By speaking so candidly and straightforwardly, Big Sister shows how little regard the family has towards Adeline's feelings and delicate kindergartener psyche. When compared to Aunt Baba's delicate handling of Adeline's questions, one can see the huge divide between Aunt Baba and the rest of the family.

The revelation that Niang is a mere seventeen years old, only eleven years Big Sister's senior, explains much of her vindictive, self-centered and often outright vicious behavior. The background into Adeline's childhood life continues to paint a picture of unwanted-ness within her own family and the general disdain of the native Chinese population in this section of China.

Mah shows how the plight of young Adeline within her own family is a microcosm for the plight of all Chinese natives in cities such as this. The final paragraph demonstrates how traditional Chinese culture, as seen in the street signs, were replaced with French culture, effectively alienating the native population, represented by Ye Ye and Nai Nai. This alienation also helped establish supremacy of the European population.

The structure of Adeline's family reflects societal standards and values, with Ye Ye and Nai Nai representing traditional Chinese people, the older siblings representing the younger, but just as looked down upon, Chinese population and Niang and the youngest siblings representing the Eurasian population and their deferential treatment.

Chinese Cinderella Chapters 4-6 Summary and Analysis

Summary

The story skips head a few months, and Tianjin is now in the middle of winter. Adeline is still in school and at this time, she and Big Sister are attending the same missionary school. Because of Big Sister's constant complaints about walking to school, they're taken everyday by the rickshaw puller, Ah-Mao. Ah-Mao is a kindly character, but is "fiercely protective" (12) of the rickshaw and won't allow anyone else to handle it. Each day after school, Big Sister takes her time getting to the rickshaw and appears to be proud of the fact that she can force Adeline and Ah-Mao to wait for her. When she finally arrives, she scowls and grows sullen, When she finally talks, it is only to quiz Adeline about her most recent school topics and slap her for not knowing something they haven't been taught and screaming about how Adeline doesn't deserve the medal she's been wearing week after week. Later that month, there is a prize ceremony at the school. No one is there to see Adeline receive her award.

At this time, Tianjin is under Japanese occupation, a terrifying experience for all of them. The Japanese soldiers demand the Chinese behave subserviently or face dire consequences. When the soldiers approach Father with a business proposal, he decides it's the perfect time to escape from Tianjin. He leaves, taking Niang and Fourth Brother with him, leaving the others in a blissful time of freedom. Their paradise is interrupted by Nai Nai's death, whereupon Father returns to take the rest of the family with him to Shanghai.

Father's homecoming is abrupt and unexpected; no one but Ye Ye had been informed about his whereabouts and his children are incredibly surprised. Instead of going on a short little outing with Ye Ye as expected, the children are whisked away by Father on a train to Shanghai with no time to say their goodbyes to Tianjin.

Ye Ye and Aunt Baba stay behind to close out their affairs, observe the hundred day mourning period of Nai Nai and take care of young Little Sister and sickly Third Brother. The rest of the siblings arrive in Shanghai, once again living "deep in the heart of the French concession" (23) in a beautiful three-story French style mansion. The period of blissful freedom has passed; Niang declares that her stepchildren are "not to invite any of [their] friends home, or visit them in their houses" (25) and are restricted to only the third floor. Big Brother remarks that they have ceased to be individuals and "have become one single unit known as all of you" (25).

Adeline is excited to return to school, this time attending Sacred Heart (Shen Xin 聖心) Missionary School, but it doesn't look like she'll make it in time since her family has once again forgotten about her existence. Luckily, she's able to catch a ride from the reluctant cook and makes it just in time. Afterschool, she is left lonely as well and with no one there to take her home, Adeline struggles to find her way in her brand new surroundings. Late in the evening, a kindly shopkeeper notices the lost little Adeline and shelters her in a restaurant until Adeline can phone home. Her family truly had forgotten about her existence and the only advice Father had to offer was to learn to read a map.

Analysis

The interactions between Adeline and her older sister serve to present the delicate relationship between the two and reinforce the "bad luck" (13) that she is to the rest of the family. Of course, Big Sister's own problems must be taken into consideration when viewing her interaction with Adeline. Big Sister's reluctance to return home hints at her troubles with Niang; though she may be favored when compared to the rest of the older siblings, she'll never garner the love and attention that Fourth Brother and Little Sister do.

Adeline and Big Sister's volatile relationship and the negative image that Adeline carries with the family is further emphasized through the lack of support during the presentation of school awards. Yen Mah's language is very matter of fact, allowing for little hope to be drawn from the situation. Of all the siblings, Adeline is the most forgotten and the most ridiculed. The language given to Big Sister also serves to position her as one of the antagonists of the novel, foreshadowing the future fickleness of her character.

Though Yen Mah's novel is a biography, many of the events in her family serve as microcosms to the overall situation of China at the time. The overbearing and intimidating Japanese presence in China is comparative to the encompassing presence of Niang in the Yen household. Though Father can escape from the presence of Japan, the children can only briefly escape from the terror of Niang and those days of blissful freedom are short lived, just like China's brief freedom from military turmoil following the end of World War II.

Nai Nai's death terminates the brief period of freedom that comes with the exit of Niang and Father. Permeating isolation, the Chinese idea of funerals and bringing things with you into the afterlife, "evaporated like an episode in a spring dream" (20), serves to show the reader that any future blissful periods for Adeline do not reflect reality. The events of the following chapters seem to build off of the sense of sorrow around the death, establishing the mood of the rest of the novel.

The family's arrival in Shanghai marks a new social structure for the older siblings. Niang's straightforward address of the siblings shows that there will be no questioning of her desires and orders and that she will not recognize the wishes of any of the siblings either. At this point, she no longer views the older siblings as individuals at all and instead refers to them as "all of you" (25), a nameless, faceless entity comprised of children she refuses to think about. By banishing them to the upper story of the house and restricting their movement, Niang does all she can to make them disappear and dispose of the reminder that Father's first wife ever existed.

Chinese Cinderella Chapters 7-10 Summary and Analysis

Summary

The family is abuzz about the rest of the Tianjin family coming to join them in Shanghai, especially since it's been six months since they've all been together. Ye Ye, Aunty Baba, Third Brother and Little Sister arrive at the house just fine, and Little Sister starts to explore. While the siblings all vie for her attention, she never strays far from Aunt Baba, even when Niang tempts her with candy. When separated from Aunt Baba by Niang, Little Sister starts to scream and struggle. After breaking Niang's pearls, Niang loses her temper, and sets about "beating her daughter in earnest" (34). While all the others look on silently, Adeline cannot restrain her cry, "Don't hurt her anymore. She is only a baby!" (35) Niang does not appreciate the outburst and declares that she "shall never forgive" (35) Adeline.

As the months stretch on, the divide between Niang's children and stepchildren widens as the older siblings are placed on a strict "austerity program" (36) and given no allowance at all. The boys are forced to sport a "Buddhist monk special" (36) haircut and are mocked by their classmates for their bald crowns. To help the children get to school, Aunt Baba and Ye Ye have been giving them enough for tram fare, but their funds have been depleted. Aunt Baba mentions she might go back to work, but Father is uncomfortable with this idea of Aunt Baba working "like a commoner" (39). If Ye Ye and Aunt Baba need an allowance, they just need to ask Niang, Adeline wonders why Ye Ye is "suddenly and mysteriously dependent on Father and Niang for pocket money" (38). When the issue of tram fare comes up, Niang is outraged that the children have gone behind her back and forbids them from troubling Aunt Baba or Ye Ye again. Soon, Adeline realizes that there is "a new family hierarchy within [the] family" (40) with Niang at the very top. Though they agree to stay loyal to Ye Ye and walk instead of buckling under Niang, one by one they slowly give in. Adeline remains resolute, walking to school in the rain and cold, though she feels isolated when her siblings are invited into the "Holy of Holies" to collect their allowances each week.

The whole house is abuzz with excitement for the New Year and the new beginnings it should bring. Traditionally, the Chinese New Year is a significant holiday full of specific rituals and all around celebration. The children are invited into the "Holy of Holies" for New Year's clothes. The brothers are given identical, loose fitting Chinese smocks while the sisters are given plain qipaos. They're outraged by the "blatant inequality" (43) between them and Niang's children, who received stylish western outfits for the New Years, and start to talk about how unfair life is. The youngest siblings have the most modern clothes, trendiest hairstyles, and unlimited access to the kitchen. They are allowed to buy anything they desire. The older siblings also complain about Niang's spies, particularly Miss Chien, the younger children's tutor. Eventually, the children attempt to get organized and revolt against

Niang, by sending a letter to Father about how unequal their treatment is. Niang catches wind of this plot, and though she does nothing initially, she invites Big Sister to the second floor and converts her into a spy. The siblings cannot remain organized without the help of Big Sister and their attempts to change the situation cease.

Adeline turns to school to keep her sane and also attempts to cheer Aunty Baba by getting good grades. Adeline's schoolmates nickname her "Genius" for her incredible dedication and intelligence. Soon, Adeline discovers writing as a means of escape from the cruelty of everyday life with Niang.

At school Adeline come to admire one of her classmates, a fiery athlete by the name of Wu Chun-mei. They strike up a fast friendship as Chun-mei lends Adeline books and in turn Adeline helps tutor her in arithmetic. Since they go home in the same direction, Chun-Mei constantly offers to take Adeline in her chauffeured car, but Adeline always refuses. Until one day, a typhoon ravages Shanghai with fierce winds and Adeline is almost swept away. She reluctantly takes a ride with Chun-mei and though Adeline never accepts a ride from her again, Chun-mei walks alongside her friend when their paths cross.

The end of World War Two starts a craze for everything American as soldiers settle into Shanghai. At this time, Chun-mei lends Adeline The Little Princess, a book about a young girl escaping poverty through hard work. This idea resonates with Adeline and she is given hope for the future. Because the war has ended, Father leaves Shanghai with Niang, Big Sister, Fourth Brother and Little Sister to reclaim his Tianjin properties, leaving the rest of the household relaxed and free. The brothers start to act like normal boys and Adeline even becomes close to Third Brother. One of Adeline's compositions wins an award in the Shanghai Newspaper Association and to congratulate her, the brothers mix her a glass or orange juice. Though she is suspicious at first, Third Brother reassures her that it's safe. When she goes to drink from it, she is hit by a "wall of urine" (69), which the boys had mixed in with the concentrate. Though the betrayal doesn't shock her, she is saddened by the way that "straddling the fence" (69) is chipping away at Third Brother's integrity. Later that week, the mischievous Chun-mei fools Adeline again: she convinces her school friends to bite into unripe persimmons.

Analysis

The conflict between Niang and Adeline is brought to a head with the latter's anger at the beating of Little Sister. This conflict will be one of the driving forces behind the rest of the novel, as evidenced by the subsequent clashes in the case of walking to school and the respect of Aunt Baba and Ye Ye. Adeline's isolation is further exemplified by her wandering around Shanghai, with her family's forgetfulness serving as a metaphor for her worthlessness to them.

For the rest of the novel, Niang uses Adeline as an outlet and a scapegoat, punishing the young girl as a way to express her frustrations and insecurities. Adeline's innocent words should not have elicited such a strong reaction from Niang, especially since Niang was in the wrong. Because Adeline exposed that Niang was not infallible in a moment of weakness, Adeline sentenced herself to a lifetime of agony.

This passage and the next establish the new family structure of the Yen household. With Nai Nai's death, Niang is new matriarch of the family and it appears as if her power is unchecked by any of the other adults, including Father. Ye Ye is no longer in the respected position that he once was, but is reduced to asking for an allowance instead of having his own funds. In the classical Chinese family structure, this is unheard of. Elders are always highly respected and sought out for advice often. Reducing Ye Ye to a mere member of the household goes against all cultural norms.

The attempt to overthrow Niang highlights the relationships between the siblings. They are united by their common complaints and the inequality that marks the household, but this is a fickle bond. Big Sister's manipulative nature comes to light once again, as she is the first to address Adeline in their attempted revolt. Though Adeline was "thrilled that Big Sister... [addressed her] personally" (45), it shows how Big Sister only acts to advance her own situation. She knows that the siblings must present themselves as a unified front to advance their cause, and must bring Adeline on board, yet the chapter before she mocked Adeline by counting the tram fare allowance on Adeline's bed.

Adeline's "Shanghai School Days" serve as a sharp relief to her home life and the everyday slights that she must suffer through. School provides Adeline with a level playing field, a place where her companions don't see her as a mother-murdering waste of space. Not only is she well-liked, but Adeline is also highly respected and seen as an equal. Through school and education, Adeline proves to herself that she should continue to live and has the potential to have a great life, even if her family is constantly bringing her down.

Chinese Cinderella Chapter 11-13 Summary and Analysis

Summary

The arrival of Mr. and Mrs. Huang—friends of Aunt Baba from Father's first marriage—has the unique consequence of the recognition of all seven children within the household. Most of the visitors only knew of the existence of Niang's two natural born children, since Niang did not want people to know she was a stepmother at her age. The Huangs have brought with them the gift of baby ducklings, one for each of the children. Adeline, naturally, was left with the scrawniest of the birds. That did not matter though, as Adeline grew to love the duckling above all else.

Named "Precious Little Treasure" (PLT for short), the duckling is especially cognizant for it's age, recognizing Adeline and following her around. Adeline tries to take special care of her duckling, finding and feeding it extra worms but is stopped by her jealous Second Brother. When trying to compensate for the loss of worms by digging in her home's garden, Adeline is attacked by Jackie, the dog. Aunt Baba sees her wound and tries to cheer Adeline up with the contents of the safe deposit box, at the same trying to prevent any waves to be kicked up. After all, Jackie is their pet. Later that night at dinner, Father wants to test out Jackie's obedience and asks for a volunteer duckling. Big Brother chooses PLT, who is then mauled by a tempted Jackie. Adeline's grief is deep, with the chapter closed off with the burial of poor Precious Little Treasure.

The book then moves on to note the mysterious disappearances of Big Sister from the household, often accompanying Father and Niang on business trips. The truth comes to light when Big Sister reveals that there are plans to marry her off to Samuel, the son of the family doctor. The age difference between the two frightens Adeline, who vows to never be married off at such an early age. Niang confiscated the gifts that started arriving, keeping the best ones for herself. This prompted Big Sister to hide the beautiful jade necklace given to her by her Great Aunt with Aunt Baba, making the latter promise to not share this news with Niang.

The wedding went off without a hitch, except for the fact that Adeline's three older brothers were thoroughly embarrassed thanks to the state of their hair and clothes. While she was in the bathroom, Adeline overheard a conversation between Niang and Great Aunt in which the existence of the jade necklace was revealed. Fearing for the fate of her sister, Adeline runs off to give some warning. Grateful, Big Sister assures her that the problem will be resolved. However, Adeline later learns that Big Sister passed the blame off onto Aunt Baba, furthering Niang's animosity towards her.

The following chapter relates the story Chun-mei's birthday party. Being one of her closest friends at school, Chun-mei invites Adeline over to celebrate her birthday.

Adeline insists that this is impossible, trying to find excuses due to her knowledge that Niang would never allow her to attend a party. However, an opportunity arises in a day off from school, special to her academy only. Since her parents don't know about her school schedule, Adeline pretends to go to school but instead attends the party.

All is going well until she has to return home for lunch. Chun-mei calls her home phone to alert her that the cake is being cut, but Niang picks up the phone. Livid, she convinces Father that Aunt Baba is a bad influence and should be separated from Adeline. Father agrees, whipping Adeline for her insolent behavior.

Analysis

These chapters serve to emphasize the disparity between Adeline and the other children within the household, even her direct siblings. The story of PLT is especially heartbreaking, with the duckling serving as a metaphor of the injustices that befall Adeline, the most "awake" member of the family. The biased selection by Big Brother and the subsequent drawn out death serve to embody the injustices of the Yen family.

At the same time, we are allowed to see some different dimensions of our characters, with Big Brother and Third Brother showing some empathy towards their younger sister. The better aspects of these characters are showcased in the waning moments of this chapter, children caught up in the fury of their imbalanced household. It is sad that we do not get to see these two characters develop much further. Although they are painted as oppressive for much of the novel, it is in scenes like this one where the reader yearns for a more detailed look at the periphery characters, perhaps not as immoral as they appear from young Adeline's point of view.

Afterwards, the scene of Big Sister's wedding juxtaposes the upscale Anglicized society that Niang's children live in and the antique customs that the natural born children are forced to uphold. The betrayal of Aunt Baba by Big Sister should not come off as a surprise to anyone reading the book, since the characters have been noticeably static. The wedge driven between Niang and Aunt Baba clearly foreshadows the impossibility of this family structure staying the way it is for long.

The cause for the disparity between the living conditions of the two sets of Yen children is again brought into question by these chapters. The embarrassment that the three eldest brothers suffer at the hands of their classmates is very public, as is their exposure to the various guests at the wedding. Since Father's prioritization of public image has been of the driving factors behind the developments thus far in the novel, his tolerance for the public shaming of his children seems oddly out of character. How can a man who cares so much of what others think of him allow his children to wear antiquated clothing? The facade of a happy and modern family that Father has worked so hard to create would seem irreparable by the events of the wedding.

The events surrounding Chun-mei's birthday party serve to highlight the injustice of the current living system in place within the household. Although Adeline does not tell the truth to her adopted mother, this small act of rebellion is a necessary act by our protagonist. The conflict between Niang and Adeline again begins to bare its teeth, showing that there is still someone who recognizes the unfairness of the situation. However, the power imbalance is again brought to light with the whipping of Adeline, reminding the reader that there is no poetic justices in this tale.

Chinese Cinderella Chapter 14-16 Summary and Analysis

Summary

The upcoming elections for class president are all the talk at Adeline's school with the two most likely candidates being Adeline and Chen Lei-Lei. On the day before the election, Adeline is worried about getting home on time so she hurries her final candidate speech in favor of her friend Chun-mei. When she gets home, Ye Ye and Aunt Baba confront her. They ask what her father told her as he whipped her. A scared Adeline chooses not to share; she instead talks about how much better her life is at school.

At school the next day, the class initiated the vote for class president and Adeline came out as winner. She is exuberant to receive this level of appreciation from her classmates, a massive honor in light of the responsibilities given to this first president. She skips back home filled with utter joy, incredulous at the successes she has accumulated at school. However, her joy is ruptured by the presence of her friends at her home, a massive violation of the Yen family rules. Niang and Father are furious at this intrusion and slap her before forcing her to kick her friends out. After this, Adeline is labeled ungrateful and told that she is to move away to a school in Tianjin.

Adeline is at first surprised to note how few people were boarding the flight to go to Tianjin, a noticeable inconsistency from the rest of the flights of Shanghai. On the flight, Father approaches Adeline and asks her for her native Chinese name, which he has forgotten. This show of disregard saddens Adeline, although she is a bit cheered up when Father allows her to share his birthday. Once they arrive in Tianjin, they drive far off into the night, arriving at some steel wrought gates that Adeline vaguely recognizes. After Niang greets the two nuns, Mother Marie and Mother Natalie, warmly, Adeline recognizes that they are at St. Joseph's, her old school.

On the next day, Adeline learns that the reason for the mass diaspora out of Tianjin is the eminent arrival of the Communist party and the PLA. This seems like an incredibly cruel fate to consign a young girl to, regardless of the rivalry that had been formed. Adeline is put in a beginning english class, the exclusive spoken tongue of St. Joseph's. In another show of her excellent work ethic, Adeline learns the language well. By December of the same year, Adeline was the only person besides the nuns left at St. Joseph. The nights of Christmas Eve and Christmas Day were particularly rough, with the nuns unable to adequately take care of the young girl. She has not yet received any letters from her family, prompting a deep sadness that is echoed in a letter she writes to Aunt Baba.

This numb back and forth is ended when Adeline hears news that her aunt has come to take her away to Hong Kong. Although originally excited by the prospect of Aunt

Baba delivered salvation, she is shocked to find her Aunt Reine Schilling, Niang's older sister. Reine and the Schillings turn out to be kind souls, very much different from the rest of her family. After updating her with news of the fall of the Nationalist Party, Reine tells her they are going to Hong Kong with the rest of the family, who will be very much surprised to see Adeline again.

The trip on the British flagship China Star is highlighted by the friendliness of Adeline's cousins, Victor and Claudine. Fair and educated, they care about making sure that Adeline has a good time and is treated equally. Adeline is stunned that the distribution of the beds inside the cabin is distributed by the drawing of lots, not by age. At night, Adeline would fantasize about being adopted by them. Although Niang does not seem angry when she sees that Adeline has returned, Adeline looks to avoid her at all costs. She is sheltered by Ye Ye before there can be greater repercussions at her arrival. Various family outings are then organized, all which leave out Adeline. Victor is quick to note this and proclaim his disapproval.

During these outings, Adeline stays home with her grandfather. While talking to him, she reflects on the importance of the Chinese language and why she should keep working to master it, regardless of her preferences for English. Ye Ye gives her a lecture on the beauty of Chinese language, imparting a great deal of knowledge onto Adeline. The next day, Adeline is again about to be left out of a large family outing. This time, Victor stands up for her and declares that he will not go. The two hang back together and Adeline is so grateful that she gives him her only book, Paper Magic.

Analysis

There is an interesting backstory to the elections for president, the greater historical theme of China being strongly influenced by the culture of their conquerors. With the United States as their benevolent overlords, China now sees the inherent superiority of democracy. The election of is particularly lucid in the context of the close allegiance between China and the United States but ironic when looking at the country's communist future.

Adeline's victory is presumed by the reader but momentous for the character herself, the first sign of confirmation that she is doing things the right way. Particularly of notice is the way her classmates look at he, admiringly. Adeline is not just another student, picked at random by a group of uncaring peers. She is the bona fide leader of a group of girls who truly care about the idea of democracy and who their leader is. In a way, the presidency serves as a metaphor for acceptance. While at home it is not achieved, she has earned it at school.

The subsequent reaction of Father and Niang is irrational and odd. Although they are clearly the antagonists of the novel, their behavior is overly villainous, and does not align with their care for appearances. The contempt shown by Chun-mei is commendable but at the end of the day worthless, like the encouragement of Ye Ye and Aunt Baba.

Adeline's flight to Tianjin is depressing on a variety of levels. First, there is the fact that her father cares so little for her that he does not remember her name or her birthdate. Secondly, the unbelievable negligence that would allow someone to abandon their child in the path of an incoming army is stunning. Finally, the imagery that surrounds a young girl, destitute and alone, spending Christmas time alone in a church is haunting. The reader's emotions are truly engaged during this chapter of Adeline's chilling life.

Finally, we get to our first true heroes of the stories, the Schillings. Sadly, they are exemplary because of how normal they are. The Schilling's actions only seem out of the ordinary because we have been exclusively exposed to the Yen family, a group not worth imitation. The humanity expressed by the Schilling, especially Victor, provide us with hope and allow for the only other characters that we can feel proud to support.

Chinese Cinderella Chapter 17-20 Summary and Analysis

Summary

The day that the Schillings leave, Niang is quick to scoop up Adeline with all of her belongings and taking her away. Fourth Brother is also in the car and treating her angrily, due to the fact that Adeline spoiled his nefarious prank to hurt Ye Ye earlier in the day, getting him in trouble with Father. After that, Ye Ye and Adeline sat together, with the former looking resigned to his fate. After going to a fancy tea with Fourth Brother and Niang, they pull up to Sacred Heart School and Orphanage. After the initial fear of being given away, Adeline is pleased to hear that will be joining the school as a boarder.

The following chapter is also short, picking the story up two years after we dropped Adeline off at Sacred Heart. She has received one of the eggs that parents usually send to the children at the school; she knows this must be a fluke considering that she has not received an egg in the two years she has attended Sacred Heart. This serves as a way to catch us with her life, as she continues to excel at school while being excluded from family life. We are reminded of her dreadful dress condition in comparison to her more affluent classmates, who were not exactly sympathetic to her troubles.

Since Sunday is visiting day, Adeline spends them in the library, engrossed in her books. One of her classmates and her mother walk in on Adeline reading King Lear and are duly impressed. Adeline uses this opportunity to express her sorrow of Ye Ye's living conditions under the thumb of Niang, as well as expressing her love of reading. The chapter ends with an overheard conversation, showing that her classmates find her an interesting personality with an inability to dress appropriately.

On the last day of term, Adeline hangs out with the last couple of friends that need to get taken home. While they are teasing each other, the girls are reminded of some interesting conversations they had in class about serendipity and galvanism. The punch line of said discussion is her chubby friend's love of frog legs and that the serendipitous event in the eighteenth century resulted in the discovery of galvanism. After others started to leave, Adeline's two closest friends (Rachel and Mary) stayed with her. Together, they made a pact to explore the world and be there for each other.

Shortly after term finished, Adeline was overwhelmed by a sickness, which turned out to be pneumonia. Her friend Mary would visit her constantly, until father's chauffeur picked her up. This, combined with Father's occasional presence, served to end the rumors around boarding school that Adeline was an orphan. Adeline was taken home and allowed to rest there for a week until she recovered from her pneumonia. There, she hangs out with Third Brother and Ye Ye. Third Brother updates Adeline on all the going ons within the family, with all the brothers heading to England for school and Big Sister staying inside of Communist China. Ye Ye speaks of how proud he is of Adeline's achievements and reprimands her when she speaks of her inability to find a way out, saying that she will create her own destiny. This bolsters her spirit, encouraging her to continue succeeding in school.

Analysis

History plays a large role in the development of the current environment that surrounds the Yen family, with the victories of the Communist Party pushing the family south. The Chinese Civil War was an ongoing struggle that was briefly supplanted by the invasion of the Japanese, pitting the Communist forces led by Mao Zedong with the Nationalist Party of Chiang Kai-shek. The affluent nature of the Yen family would probably align them more with the latter, which was losing the war. This forced their move to Hong Kong.

Although these three chapters are brutally short, they serve to highlight the most admirable aspects of Adeline's character while again bringing forth the challenges she faces. Her departure from her home may have been sudden but it was not entirely unwelcome; Adeline understands that life at a boarding school is much better than having to live with Niang for any period of time. The irony of year-round school being considered heavenly is not lost on the reader.

Adeline's years at Sacred Heart have allowed her to flourish academically, pushing her up grades faster than anyone else. Though this brings out the contempt of some of her peers, she has also gained the admiration of a good number of others. While not outwardly admired, she has gained a place in her school. At the same time, Adeline is still considered an outcast because of her lack of family and the poor state of her clothes and hair. The mood at Sacred Heart, although still a bit gloomy from Adeline's perspective, is much brighter than that of the earlier chapters. Perhaps we are meant to see that, as she grows more independent, life becomes better for Adeline.

Chapter 19 does not have much purpose besides establishing some sense of friendship between Adeline and her peers at Sacred Heart. All the friendly back and forth serves to reestablish school as the main form of escape for Adeline, an arena under which she can excel and stand out. The promise that she and her fiends will support each other till the end is endearing. It promises a way out for this long-suffering girl.

The following chapter serves a purpose as means to update us on the progress of family affairs. The reader learns of the possibility of school in England from Third Brother, an opportunity that seems perfect for a student like Adeline seeking escape. At the same time, we see that Ye Ye is nearing the end of is battle. The introduction of diabetes, combined with the defeated way that he carries himself, foreshadows the tragic events of the next chapter.

Chinese Cinderella Chapter 21-22 Summary and Analysis

Summary

Since the holidays were not yet over, Adeline had to spend a lot of time by herself at Sacred Heart. Suddenly, she is smitten by the idea of taking part in a playwriting competition that is open to students from around the world. Although she is afraid, Mother Louisa encourages her to take the shot. She receives her first piece of mail, the instructions on how to take part, soon after. Although she continuously writes to Niang and her Father on the topic of attending school in England, it seems like they have forgotten about her even more. Meanwhile, she continues to wait for an answer from the playwriting competition.

As she is playing basketball later on in the year, Adeline is called over by one of the nuns. Though at first she thinks she is going home, she is instead told she is being taken to her Ye Ye's funeral. Adeline sobs throughout, while the rest of her family looks on stoically. Niang loudly proclaims that Adeline is looking ever more ugly as she grows older, hurting Adeline at a moment of great weakness. Niang then tells her that she needs to find a job, since Father could not support her fourteen-year-old self forever. In a turn of events, Adeline returns to school to find out that her friends have found her to be the most likely to succeed.

However, the combination of Ye Ye's death and Niang's proclamation that she must leave school and find a job had left Adeline in a state of depression. Avoiding her classmates and dinner, the only thing she had to look forward to were the results of the playwriting competition. One Saturday, eight weeks away from the end of school, Adeline is called back to her house. Brought directly to father, Adeline is afraid that she will be married off. Instead, Father expresses his great pride in her victory in the International Playwriting Competition, an award pointed out to her by his work acquaintance. In his state of pride and jubilance, Father agrees to allow her to go to school in England to become an obstetrician. Adeline is overjoyed.

The final chapter is a letter from Aunt Baba, expressing her love and admiration of Adeline's success. She wants Adeline to know that she loves her very much and that she will always hold her "precious in my heart." Afterwards, she shares the Chinese folk tale that is similar to that of Cinderella. She hopes that his story will serve as a talisman against despair. She ends by telling Adeline that her future is limitless and that she will always be proud of her, her Chinese Cinderella.

Analysis

The final chapters of Chinese Cinderella serve as the climax, the falling action, and the conclusion all in one. The tragic death of Ye Ye has long been in the cards, yet it does not provide the sort of repercussions that one would expect from the death of such a monumental character. This perhaps serves to reflect the lack of impact that Ye Ye was able to have on the development of his granddaughter, the final harsh truth of the Yen patriarch.

Niang's ultimatum in regards to Adeline needing to find a job install a sense of urgency in these last few chapters. However, the response from the playwriting competition seems imminent, a Chekov's gun poised to go off. At the same time, the dark nature of the novel so far has let doubt creep into the mind of the reader. The positive resolution is at once expected, yet seems too much like the fairytale ending that this story tends away from.

The ride to her new house, one that she only learned existed in passing, is tense. Neither her nor any of the characters that she interacts with on the way seem to be aware of her fate. Yen Mah creates a setting that contradicts the tense mood, the sound of splashing water and peaceful streams of light described by father being the prominent images in the reader's mind.

Father's decision to allow Adeline to attend school in England may seem at first to be the work of a finally enlightened man. However, the astute reader will see that this is just a continuation of Father's banal pride, a happiness that comes only when his peers are impressed. Regardless, the end result is the same: Adeline gets to make a name for herself.

Aunt Baba's letter is a nice not for the book to end with. One of Adeline's protectors can finally be heard from, yet she expresses the same support that she has before. While support continues to be nice, it is not the tangible change that Adeline needed throughout her life. The letter remains a touching notion, as well as the sharing of the story of the Chinese Cinderella, passed down from Adeline's mysterious mother to Aunt Baba and now to her. Although there are many questions that remain to be asked in terms of the motives of some of our characters, the fact that justice finally befalls Adeline is satisfaction enough.

Chinese Cinderella The Falling Leaves Foundation

Adeline Yen Mah is Founder and President of the Falling Leaves Foundation, whose mission is 'to promote understanding between East and West' and provides funds for the study of Chinese history, language, and culture. There is also a website dedicated to teaching Chinese over the Internet for free, and the foundation has established a poetry prize at UCLA. Chinese Character A Day is Adeline Yen Mah's dream to teach mandarin Chinese to anyone who wishes to learn. Students are able to type Chinese characters on their home computers after the first lesson. The lessons are based on her book, "China Land of Dragons and Emperors", which is a free download for new email subscribers. From then on, Adeline teaches students how to recognize, type, pronounce, and write Chinese Characters. Adeline also created this site under the belief that China will probably become the world's largest economy in twenty years' time. Knowing Chinese will not only provide an understanding of China's history and culture, it will also "create endless opportunities for a brilliant future."

Chinese Cinderella Links

Chinese Character a Day

http://chinesecharacteraday.com/

The educational site provided by Adeline Yen Mah's foundation, meant to expand knowledge of the Chinese language and culture.

Adeline Yen Mah's Official Website

http://www.adelineyenmah.com/

Contains a lot of information about the author and her novels, including links to outside reviews.

Timeline of Yen Mah's life

http://www.timetoast.com/timelines/adeline-yen-mah-biography

Helpful timeline depicting the major events of Adeline's life.

BBC piece on Adeline Yen Mah

http://www.bbc.co.uk/worldservice/learningenglish/movingwords/celebritychoice/adelineyenmah.shtml

A segment as part of a larger BBC series focusing on the teachings and accomplishments of Adeline Yen Mah.

Story of Chinese Cinderella (original Chinese myth)

http://www.myseveralworlds.com/2007/08/02/yeh-shen-the-chinese-cinderella/

To use as a reference throughout the novel: the *Chinese Cinderella* story to which the title refers.

Chinese Cinderella Essay Questions

1. **What makes the events that occurred during her childhood so poignant to Ms. Yen Mah at the point of her life when she relates the story?**

   A complete answer to this question would look at a it from a variety of perspectives. While one can talk about the deep psychological trauma that events cause during a decisively absorbent age, it is also important to mention the imperfectness of memory. The thoughts of a child can be distorted with time, augmenting some wrongs and forgetting some rights. The most important aspect of an effective response is the ability to understand different perspectives.

2. **How might Adeline's relatives describe themselves if given the chance to tell their own life stories?**

   An effective answer to this question would look to address the incredibly static nature of the characters within Adeline's story. None of the characters within the novel, besides perhaps Adeline herself, have any changes in personality, either positive or negative. They are, at the end of the novel, the same people as they were at the beginning. The writer would first look to answer the question of why the characters are so static. Then, they would look to find the deeper conflicts that may have affected the development of these periphery characters.

3. **Why does Niang behave towards Adeline, and her other stepchildren, as she does?**

   A difficult but central question, the nature of Niang's conflict with Joseph's natural born children can be difficult to ascertain. The matter of Niang's youth is a particularly interesting aspect for the writer to pursue, although it will not serve as a satisfactory answer on its own. The successful essay will also look at the dynamic between Niang and her husband, perhaps trying to answer why he deferred to her so easily. Father's pride of his French wife may perhaps be the root of this development. Finally, the matter of inheritance may be considered as in play.

4. **At one point, Adeline feels close to her third brother. However, the bond is constantly broken and rebuilt throughout the story. Why is this relationship difficult and changeable?**

   As the least confrontational of the siblings, Third Brother is naturally the one who Adeline can build the greatest connection with. However, the flippant nature of his alliances can also brig about a rapid end to any comradeship. While Third Brother may perhaps like his younger sister, he does not have a strong enough personality to stand up to his other siblings. An above average essay will try to explain the origins of this dynamic and try to explain how the distinct prerequisites under which those moments of friendship arise.

5. **Why doesn't Aunt Baba do more to 'rescue' Adeline?**

   A prickly issue to address, the answer to this question would probably characterize Aunt Baba as a very passive sort of hero, a benevolent human rather than a game changing force. Although this would go against the role of protagonist she takes in the novel, it is by far the most realistic. A successful essay will look at Aunt Baba as someone forced into the hero role since she was the only one who would help Adeline, but unable to complete the prerequisites of the elevated position. Aunt Baba does what her personality has dictated she could do: she writes encouraging letters and prays for her niece, not charging into a boarding school and flying her out to America.

6. **How does the financial state of Adeline's family influence the dynamics of the story?**

   An observant reader would try to visualize a life in which Adeline's family was unable to obtain the resources it had, closer to the beggars mentioned throughout the book. A particularly interesting position would say that even though Adeline had an incredibly difficult childhood, she had access to opportunities that millions of Chinese children did not. If things had been different and the Yen family could not afford mansions and American cars, Adeline may not have even been born. This is an interesting essay topic because it challenges the writer to think that maybe the term of "Chinese Cinderella" may fit others better than Adeline Yen Mah.

7. **How does Chinese culture play a role in Adeline's life?**

   The important distinction to take note of here is the difference between the dynamic of Adeline's family and a more traditional Chinese family. Although there is the customary nod to major public holidays, the Yen family is distinctly anglicized. The writer can perhaps engage with the question of whether this is a shift throughout Chinese society or if it is an issue particular to the Yens. While the role of Chinese culture is not direct, the successful essay would note that it's influence is pervasive all the way until it is stated outright in Ye Ye's last monologue.

8. **Nai Nai has had her feet bound as a child. This 'custom' is part of an older time. Culturally, the world of Adeline and that of her grandparents are very different. From Adeline's story, what can you see that has changed and what has stayed the same over time?**

The successful essay writer would note the similarities in terms of what is expected from each of the sexes but the differences in the process. While women in Adeline's time have more opportunities than before, they are expected to play a role similar to that in the times of footbinding. It will be important to note the specific aspects of Adeline's story that tie back, like the arranged marriages and the ability of her to study abroad. However, it will be crucial to note counterexamples within the novel.

9. **How does the political climate of the time affect the development of Adeline's story?**

   Adeline lives in the midst of major changes in Chinese society, with the upcoming victory of the People's Liberation Army bringing about massive governmental evolution. However, it seems like the primary impact that this has on Adeline is on her location, not her personality. There are two ways the writer may take this. For one, he can say that national politics have little effect on the day to day lives of the people, particularly in a family as affluent as the Yens. On the other hand, the writer may question the reliability of the narrator, since Adeline may not be able to grasp how the rise of the Communist party affected her parent's personal development and thus the growth of their children.

10. **Does the title of 'Chinese Cinderella' truly fit Adeline Yah, or is this an inaccurate view of her life?**

    There are many dimensions to a question of this magnitude, which must be made to fit under the banners of "yes" and "no". The argument on the side of "yes" would point to the cruelty of her adopted stepmother and the self-reliance that created the opportunities that she had today. The stereotypical "no" side would point to the wealth of the Yen family and the opportunities this afforded her, which would arguably outweigh the personal difficulties that she had to overcome. However, a exceptional "no" essay would not focus on the wealth aspect but rather on how the self-reliant aspect of Adeline's story makes her very different from Cinderella, both Chinese and Western.

Chinese Cinderella Quizzes

1. **How old is Adeline at the beginning of the novel?**
   A. Seven years old
   B. Four years old
   C. Five years old
   D. Nine years old

2. **What is the name of the school Adeline attends in Hong Kong?**
   A. Sacred Heart
   B. St. Lawrence Martyr
   C. Christ the Redeemer
   D. Saint Joseph's

3. **What is the name of the leader of the People's Liberation Army?**
   A. Hu Jintao
   B. Li Si
   C. Kim Il-Sung
   D. Mao Zedong

4. **Who was the leader of the Nationalist Party?**
   A. Chiang Kai-shek
   B. Mao Fumei
   C. Ch'en Chien-ju
   D. Mao Zedong

5. **What is the english name of Adeline's Big Sister?**
   A. Mary
   B. Elizabeth
   C. Linda
   D. Lydia

6. **What is the english name of Adeline's Big Brother?**
   A. Gray
   B. Gregory
   C. Grant
   D. George

7. **What is the english name of Adeline's Third Brother?**
   A. James
   B. Michael
   C. Jim
   D. Carl

8. **What is the english name of Adeline's Second Brother?**
   A. Mark
   B. James
   C. Edgar
   D. Thomas

9. **What is the english name of Fourth Younger Brother?**
   A. Florence
   B. Fred
   C. Franklin
   D. Frank

10. **What does Niang tell Adeline after Ye Ye's funeral?**
   A. That she is no longer welcome
   B. That she will now have Ye Ye's room
   C. That she must get a job
   D. That she respects her effort

11. **What is the english name of Little Sister?**
   A. Camila
   B. Susan
   C. Silvia
   D. Alyssa

12. **Which one of these is NOT a language that Ye Ye predicts will remain in the future?**
   A. Chinese
   B. Spanish
   C. French
   D. English

13. **What does Niang demand from the children in exchange for tram fare?**
   A. A sincere apology denouncing Ye Ye's actions
   B. Healthier eating
   C. Perfect grades
   D. More chores

14. **What book is Adeline reading when she is surprised by her classmate and her mother in the library?**
   A. Master and the Margarita
   B. Moby Dick
   C. King Lear
   D. Romeo and Juliet

15. **How old is Niang when she marries Father?**
A. 17
B. 14
C. 25
D. 21

16. **What happens to the best presents Big Sister receives at her wedding?**
A. They are given as an offering to the nearest Buddhist temple
B. They are given to Ye Ye
C. Big Sister's husband sells them
D. Niang takes them

17. **For what holiday do the children receive new clothing?**
A. Chinese New Year
B. Chinese Independence Day
C. Yom Kippur
D. Hinanatsuri

18. **What was the name of the book that Adeline borrowed from her schoolfriend?**
A. The Tao of Pooh
B. Simple Magic Tricks
C. The Secret Garden
D. The Little Princess

19. **What was Niang's nationality?**
A. French
B. English
C. Japanese
D. French-Chinese

20. **Who was invading Tianjin while Adeline boarded with the nuns?**
A. The Nationalist Army
B. The Japanese Army
C. The People's Liberation Army
D. United States Marines

21. **Which famous Shakespearean character does Adeline compare Ye Ye to?**
A. King Lear
B. MacBeth
C. Romeo
D. Horatio

22. **Who drove the rickshaw in Tianjin?**
    A. Sheng
    B. Lin
    C. Chin-Meh
    D. Ah-Mao

23. **What year does World War Two end?**
    A. 1933
    B. 1952
    C. 1940
    D. 1945

24. **Where does Aunt Baba put Adeline's report cards?**
    A. In the dresser
    B. In her safe deposit box
    C. Under her bed
    D. In her closet

25. **What happened to all the pictures of Adeline's mother?**
    A. Her father ordered that they be destroyed shortly after Nai Nai's funeral
    B. Niang tore them all up
    C. They decayed with age, since they were not preserved
    D. Aunt Baba stole them all

Quiz 1 Answer Key

1. **(B)** Four years old
2. **(A)** Sacred Heart
3. **(D)** Mao Zedong
4. **(A)** Chiang Kai-shek
5. **(D)** Lydia
6. **(B)** Gregory
7. **(A)** James
8. **(C)** Edgar
9. **(C)** Franklin
10. **(C)** That she must get a job
11. **(B)** Susan
12. **(C)** French
13. **(A)** A sincere apology denouncing Ye Ye's actions
14. **(C)** King Lear
15. **(A)** 17
16. **(D)** Niang takes them
17. **(A)** Chinese New Year
18. **(D)** The Little Princess
19. **(D)** French-Chinese
20. **(C)** The People's Liberation Army
21. **(A)** King Lear
22. **(D)** Ah-Mao
23. **(D)** 1945
24. **(B)** In her safe deposit box
25. **(A)** Her father ordered that they be destroyed shortly after Nai Nai's funeral

Chinese Cinderella Quizzes

1. **What is the age difference between Niang and Big Sister?**
   A. Six years
   B. Twenty-three years
   C. Seventeen years
   D. Eleven years

2. **What event spurred Father's departure from Tianjin to Shanghai?**
   A. Ye Ye wanted to move the family business
   B. The Japanese wanted to become business partners
   C. Niang no longer liked living in Tianjin
   D. Nai Nai's death made it too difficult to stay

3. **What were the streets in the Tianjin French concession named after?**
   A. French Generals
   B. Chinese legendary figures
   C. Catholic Saints
   D. Famous battles

4. **In Tianjin, what was the unspoken signal that no Chinese were welcome (except for Chinese nannies of European children)?**
   A. Segregated facilities
   B. The signs were entirely in French with no Chinese translation
   C. Signs in windows stated "no Chinese"
   D. Upscale eurasian neighborhoods

5. **What is Adeline's favorite fruit?**
   A. Cherries
   B. Dragon eyes
   C. Fuyu persimmons
   D. Apples

6. **How does Adeline earn the medal in kindergarten?**
   A. She wins a composition compotition
   B. She leads the class for a week
   C. She has the highest scores in everything, except for art
   D. She's just that awesome

7. **When does Father first speak to Adeline?**
   A. He calls her to as where she is in the sixth chapter
   B. He tells her that she'll look fine in her qipao in the ninth chapter
   C. He tells her she has no time to pack on their way to Shanghai in the fifth chapter
   D. He comments on her medal at dinner in the third chapter

8. **What floor are the older siblings confined to?**
   A. The servant's quarters
   B. The second floor
   C. The "Holy of Holies"
   D. The third floor

9. **Who stays behind in Tianjin when the family moves to Shanghai?**
   A. Ye Ye, Aunt Baba, Third Brother and Little Sister
   B. Ye Ye, Fourth Brother and Big Sister
   C. Aunt Baba, Fourth Brother and Little Sister
   D. Ye Ye and Aunt Baba

10. **What does Adeline name her duck?**
    A. Precious Little Treasure
    B. Sacred Heart
    C. Precocious, Loving Duck
    D. Pretty Young Thing

11. **How does Adeline's duck die?**
    A. The duck catches a cold
    B. Her duck is placed in front of Jackie to show off Jackie's obedience training
    C. Second Brother is jealous of the special treatment she shows her duck and snaps the duck's neck
    D. The cook makes it into duck soup

12. **Who does Big Sister marry?**
    A. Ah-mao
    B. Samuel Sung
    C. Mah Li-suh
    D. Wu Chun-li

13. **Why do the girls at Sacred Heart get a holiday on Monday?**
    A. It is the spring festival
    B. It is the end of World War Two
    C. It is Chinese Independence Day
    D. It is the new Mother Superior's name day

14. **Why is Adeline wary of Chun-mei's dog?**
    A. Her family's dog, Jackie, bit her
    B. Pugs are gross
    C. She has always had an aversion to dogs
    D. She's more of a duck person

15. **Who does Adeline run against in the class election?**
A. Wu Chun-mei
B. Big Sister
C. Yen Jun-li
D. Chen Lei-lei

16. **When Adeline returns to Tianjin, why is it sparsely populated?**
A. The People's Liberation Army is about to invade
B. An outbreak of the flu has overcome the city
C. Tianjin is no longer an attractive city
D. There is rumor of a revolution by the French concession

17. **What birthday does Father decide to give Adeline after forgetting hers?**
A. Aunty Baba's
B. Her mother's
C. His own
D. Niang's

18. **What school did Adeline and Niang share?**
A. Sacred Heart Elementary
B. St. Joseph's
C. St. Cathrine's
D. Sacred Heart High School

19. **Where does Aunt Baba work in Shanghai?**
A. At a restaurant
B. Housekeeping at the mansion
C. At Great Aunt's bank
D. At the French concession

20. **What picture does Aunt Baba have in her safe deposit box?**
A. A picture of Ye Ye and Nai Nai's wedding
B. A picture of Adeline's mother
C. A picture of Aunt Baba and Father as children
D. A picture of Adeline

21. **Why does Adeline accept a ride from Wu Chun-mei?**
A. There were sketchy characters wandering the streets of Shanghai
B. She is almost blown away by a typhoon
C. She was held at gunpoint
D. They were let out late from school and Adeline was worried about being home late

22. **How does Nai Nai die?**
    A. Niang poisons her
    B. She has an aneurysm in the tub
    C. She drowns
    D. Her arthritis makes her fall down the stairs

23. **How does Adeline react when Second Brother comes to the table?**
    A. She hides under the table
    B. She's happy to be joined by her favorite brother
    C. She cringes
    D. She is wary

24. **What is Big Sister's handicap?**
    A. She is not very bright
    B. She was born with a lame arm
    C. She has a club foot
    D. She has a heart murmur

25. **Why does Big Sister slap Adeline?**
    A. Ah-mao made a comment about Big Sister
    B. Big Sister thinks Adeline's face would look better slapped
    C. Adeline is not moving fast enough
    D. Adeline is not able to answer Big Sister's questions

Quiz 2 Answer Key

1. **(D)** Eleven years
2. **(B)** The Japanese wanted to become business partners
3. **(C)** Catholic Saints
4. **(B)** The signs were entirely in French with no Chinese translation
5. **(B)** Dragon eyes
6. **(B)** She leads the class for a week
7. **(D)** He comments on her medal at dinner in the third chapter
8. **(D)** The third floor
9. **(A)** Ye Ye, Aunt Baba, Third Brother and Little Sister
10. **(A)** Precious Little Treasure
11. **(B)** Her duck is placed in front of Jackie to show off Jackie's obedience training
12. **(B)** Samuel Sung
13. **(D)** It is the new Mother Superior's name day
14. **(A)** Her family's dog, Jackie, bit her
15. **(D)** Chen Lei-lei
16. **(A)** The People's Liberation Army is about to invade
17. **(C)** His own
18. **(B)** St. Joseph's
19. **(C)** At Great Aunt's bank
20. **(A)** A picture of Ye Ye and Nai Nai's wedding
21. **(B)** She is almost blown away by a typhoon
22. **(B)** She has an aneurysm in the tub
23. **(C)** She cringes
24. **(B)** She was born with a lame arm
25. **(D)** Adeline is not able to answer Big Sister's questions

Chinese Cinderella Quizzes

1. **Why do people laugh at Adeline at the prize giving ceremony in Tianjin?**
   A. She trips on her way to the stage
   B. No one is there to celebrate with her
   C. Her skirt is crooked
   D. Adeline is not tall enough to walk up the stairs and must climb

2. **Why do Ye Ye and Aunt Baba stay behind in Tianjin?**
   A. They want to observe the hundred days of mourning for Nai Nai
   B. They need to settle their affairs
   C. Fourth Brother is too young to travel
   D. They aren't ready to go to Shanghai

3. **Who says, "we have become one single unit known as all of you?"**
   A. Fourth Brother
   B. Big Sister
   C. Adeline
   D. Big Brother

4. **Why does Adeline decide to learn how to read maps?**
   A. Big Brother has lots of maps
   B. Aunt Baba suggests it
   C. Ye Ye says that map reading is an essential skill
   D. She realizes she cannot rely on anyone to look out for her

5. **What school does Adeline attend in Shanghai?**
   A. St. Joseph's
   B. St. John's Seminary
   C. Sacred Heart Missionary School
   D. Immaculate Heart

6. **What does Little Sister break upon her homecoming?**
   A. A candy dish
   B. Niang's pearls
   C. Niang's heart
   D. Aunt Baba's blouse

7. **What do the older brothers call their short haircuts?**
   A. The "Baldie"
   B. The "Buddhist Monk Special"
   C. The "Lightbulb"
   D. The "Too Short, Not Sweet"

8. **What is Adeline doing when she hears of Ye Ye's death?**
   A. Working on a composition for him
   B. Writing a letter to Aunt Baba
   C. Reading
   D. Playing basketball

9. **What gift from Grand Aunt does Big Sister want to keep for herself?**
   A. Makeup
   B. A jade necklace
   C. A jade ring
   D. A beautiful qipao

10. **Who does Big Sister accuse of keeping the jade pendant away from Niang?**
   A. Her husband
   B. Aunt Baba
   C. Adeline
   D. Great Aunt

11. **How does Adeline keep I[The Little Princess] with her, even after she returns the book?**
   A. She asks Aunt Baba to buy a copy for her
   B. She steals a copy from the bookstore
   C. She memorizes the entire book
   D. She copies out pages and commits pieces to memory

12. **Who brings ducklings for the children?**
   A. The Huangs
   B. Ye Ye
   C. The Schillings
   D. Ah-mao

13. **Why does Father agree to send Adeline to school in England?**
   A. She wins a writing competition and her name is in the paper
   B. She wants to be a doctor
   C. She has done so well in school, that her father thinks it a shame not to let her continue
   D. Father cannot find a suitor for her at this time

14. **How long are communications between Aunt Baba and Adeline severed?**
   A. Four years
   B. Six months
   C. Three months
   D. Two years

15. **What was the name of the Chinese Cinderella?**
A. Jun-lin
B. Cinderella
C. Ye Xian
D. Yen Ling

16. **Who helps Adeline burry her duck?**
A. Ye Ye
B. Little Sister
C. Third Brother
D. Aunt Baba

17. **How did the Yens know Samuel Sung?**
A. He was a neighbor in Shanghai
B. His father, Dr. Sung was Nai Nai's old doctor
C. They found him through a matchmaker
D. He attended Big Sister's school

18. **What was the age difference between Big Sister and her husband?**
A. Fifteen years
B. Twenty years
C. Twelve years
D. Two years

19. **What accent does Grand Aunt have?**
A. Ningpo
B. Shanghai
C. Mandarin
D. Tianjin

20. **How does Father punish Adeline for attending the birthday party?**
A. He forbids her from going to school
B. He takes away her duck
C. He whips her and separates her from Aunt Baba
D. He slaps her repeatedly

21. **How are head girls at Shen Xin Primary School decided upon?**
A. They have an athletic competition to decide
B. The headmistress decides
C. They poll the school
D. The sixth form class nominates and elects the head girl

22. **How many girls run for class president?**
A. Two
B. Five
C. Three
D. Nine

23. **Why do Adeline's friends come to her house?**
A. To ask her a homework question
B. To celebrate winning the election
C. To find out where she lives
D. To bring her back to Chun-mei's party

24. **When does Adeline leave from Shanghai for Tianjin?**
A. In the middle of summer
B. After Chun-mei's party
C. The day after she wins the class election
D. Once the war ends

25. **In what dynasty were Adeline's grandparents born?**
A. The Quing Dynasty
B. When Mao Zedong was in power
C. The Yuan Dynasty
D. The Ming Dynasty

Quiz 3 Answer Key

1. **(D)** Adeline is not tall enough to walk up the stairs and must climb
2. **(A)** They want to observe the hundred days of mourning for Nai Nai
3. **(D)** Big Brother
4. **(D)** She realizes she cannot rely on anyone to look out for her
5. **(C)** Sacred Heart Missionary School
6. **(B)** Niang's pearls
7. **(B)** The "Buddhist Monk Special"
8. **(D)** Playing basketball
9. **(B)** A jade necklace
10. **(B)** Aunt Baba
11. **(D)** She copies out pages and commits pieces to memory
12. **(A)** The Huangs
13. **(A)** She wins a writing competition and her name is in the paper
14. **(A)** Four years
15. **(C)** Ye Xian
16. **(C)** Third Brother
17. **(B)** His father, Dr. Sung was Nai Nai's old doctor
18. **(A)** Fifteen years
19. **(A)** Ningpo
20. **(C)** He whips her and separates her from Aunt Baba
21. **(D)** The sixth form class nominates and elects the head girl
22. **(B)** Five
23. **(B)** To celebrate winning the election
24. **(C)** The day after she wins the class election
25. **(A)** The Quing Dynasty

Chinese Cinderella Quizzes

1. **What does Father believe Adeline's Chinese name is before asking her?**
   A. Mei-li
   B. Jing-tsu
   C. Jun-len
   D. Jun-quing

2. **Who meets Adeline at the Tianjin airport?**
   A. Aunt Baba
   B. The Schillings
   C. Pierre Prosperi, Niang's brother
   D. Sister Mary

3. **What language is forbidden at St. Joseph's?**
   A. Shanghainese
   B. Any Chinese dialect
   C. English
   D. French

4. **What book does Mother Marie give Adeline for Christmas?**
   A. King Lear
   B. Paper Magic: Playing Solitary Games with Paper
   C. The Art of War
   D. The Little Princess

5. **How old are the Schilling children when Adeline sails with them?**
   A. Claudine is ten and Victor is seven
   B. Claudine is eight and Victor is eleven
   C. Claudine is nine and Victor is ten
   D. Claudine is thirteen and Victor is twelve

6. **How do the Schillings decide who gets the cot?**
   A. Adeline gets it
   B. They play rock-paper-scissors for it
   C. They draw straws
   D. They have an arithmatic competition

7. **What is Adeline's favorite part of the ship?**
   A. The aft
   B. The library
   C. The sea breeze
   D. The lifeboats

8. **What does Aunt Reine smuggle into Hong Kong?**
   A. The family
   B. Adeline
   C. Pearls
   D. Niang's diamond collection

9. **Where did the Schillings go to from Hong Kong**
   A. Shanghai
   B. America
   C. Geneva
   D. Tianjin

10. **What sad sight does Adeline see on the way to her new boarding school?**
    A. A young girl for sale
    B. A dead duck
    C. A dying beggar woman
    D. A lonely old man

11. **When Adeline first arrives at Sacred Heart School and Orphanage, what does she think will happen?**
    A. Niang is planning for Little Sister's future
    B. She'll be abandoned at the orphanage
    C. She'll be able to continue her educaiton
    D. They're going to adopt a young girl

12. **Why does Adeline receive and egg on Sunday?**
    A. A girl changed the number on her egg to Adeline's number
    B. The nuns took pity on her
    C. One of her friends smuggled in an egg for her
    D. Her parents bought her an egg

13. **What is Adeline's nickname at Sacred Heart Boarding School?**
    A. Loner
    B. Scholar
    C. Brains
    D. Genius

14. **Who is Adeline's school rival at Sacred Heart Boarding School?**
    A. Irene Tan
    B. Elanor Lui
    C. Monica Lim
    D. Wu Chun-mei

15. **What was the nickname of Mother Valentino**

A. Horse Face
B. Slowpoke
C. Super Strict
D. Scary Superior

16. **What was the connection Eleanor found between serendipity and galvanism?**

A. She said that Luigi Galvani was eating frogs legs when he bit a nerve, causing the legs to twitch
B. She said Luigi Galvani was hanging frogs on a copper wire when they twitched
C. She said the concepts had nothing to do with one another
D. She said that Luigi Galvani was dissecting frogs when he notices the legs twitching

17. **What disease did Adeline contract while at Sacred Heart?**

A. Cholera
B. Polio
C. Black Plague
D. Pneumonia

18. **What is the name of the friend who visits Adeline at the hospital?**

A. Maria
B. Amy
C. Mary
D. Rebecca

19. **With whom does Adeline make a pact with after being left behind at the boarding school?**

A. Rachel Yu and May Suen
B. Eleanor Liu and Irene Tan
C. Chun-mei Wu
D. Monica Lim

20. **Who cries at Ye Ye's funeral?**

A. Fourth Brother and Adeline
B. Adeline and Father
C. Only Adeline
D. Father, Aunt Baba and Third Brother

21. **What is the name of the hotel that Fourth Brother, Niang, and Adeline get tea at?**

A. Peninsula Hotel
B. Bates Hotel
C. Tipton Hotel
D. Commodore Hotel

22. **What is the name of the author's current husband?**
    A. Steve
    B. Pablo
    C. Bruce
    D. Bob

23. **Where did Adeline attend school in England?**
    A. Oxford University
    B. King's College
    C. University College and London Hospital Medical College
    D. Cambridge University

24. **What does Adeline believe her best feature is**
    A. Eyes
    B. Intelligence
    C. Sincerity
    D. Nothing

25. **Who does Aunt Baba live with at the end of the novel?**
    A. Great Aunt
    B. Big Sister
    C. Jackie
    D. Miss Chien

Quiz 4 Answer Key

1. **(D)** Jun-quing
2. **(C)** Pierre Prosperi, Niang's brother
3. **(B)** Any Chinese dialect
4. **(B)** Paper Magic: Playing Solitary Games with Paper
5. **(C)** Claudine is nine and Victor is ten
6. **(C)** They draw straws
7. **(B)** The library
8. **(D)** Niang's diamond collection
9. **(C)** Geneva
10. **(A)** A young girl for sale
11. **(B)** She'll be abandoned at the orphanage
12. **(A)** A girl changed the number on her egg to Adeline's number
13. **(B)** Scholar
14. **(C)** Monica Lim
15. **(A)** Horse Face
16. **(A)** She said that Luigi Galvani was eating frogs legs when he bit a nerve, causing the legs to twitch
17. **(D)** Pneumonia
18. **(C)** Mary
19. **(A)** Rachel Yu and May Suen
20. **(C)** Only Adeline
21. **(A)** Peninsula Hotel
22. **(D)** Bob
23. **(C)** University College and London Hospital Medical College
24. **(D)** Nothing
25. **(D)** Miss Chien

Chinese Cinderella Bibliography

Nicolas P. Rossenblum, author of ClassicNote. Completed on May 16, 2014, copyright held by GradeSaver.

Updated and revised by Aaron Suduiko May 25, 2015. Copyright held by GradeSaver.

Adeline Yen Mah. Falling Leaves. New York: Broadway Books, 1999.

Adeline Yen Mah. Chinese Cinderella. New York: Ember, 2010.

Susan Elkins. "An Interview with Adeline Yen Mah." amazon.co.uk. 2012-06-11. 2014-05-16. <http://www.amazon.co.uk/gp/feature.html?ie=UTF8&docId=114025>.

BBC World Sevice. "Moving Words-Adeline Yen Mah." British Broadcasting Company. 2014-05-12. <http://www.bbc.co.uk/worldservice/learningenglish/movingwords/celebritychoice/adelineyenmah.shtml>.

Writers Write. "Interview with Adeline Yen Mah." 2014-05-20. <http:www.writerswrite.com/childrens/yenma.htm>.

"Adeline Yen Mah." 2014-05-12. <http://www.adelineyenmah.com/>.

"Chinese Character a Day." 2014-05-21. <http://chinesecharacteraday.com/>.

Made in the USA
Middletown, DE
06 November 2019